John Smith

English Explorer and Colonist

Colonial Leaders

Lord Baltimore *English Politician and Colonist*

Benjamin Banneker *American Mathematician and Astronomer*

William Bradford *Governor of Plymouth Colony*

Benjamin Franklin *American Statesman, Scientist, and Writer*

Anne Hutchinson *Religious Leader*

Cotton Mather *Author, Clergyman, and Scholar*

William Penn *Founder of Democracy*

John Smith *English Explorer and Colonist*

Miles Standish *Plymouth Colony Leader*

Peter Stuyvesant *Dutch Military Leader*

Revolutionary War Leaders

Benedict Arnold *Traitor to the Cause*

Nathan Hale *Revolutionary Hero*

Alexander Hamilton *First U.S. Secretary of the Treasury*

Patrick Henry *American Statesman and Speaker*

Thomas Jefferson *Author of the Declaration of Independence*

John Paul Jones *Father of the U.S. Navy*

Thomas Paine *Political Writer*

Paul Revere *American Patriot*

Betsy Ross *American Patriot*

George Washington *First U.S. President*

John Smith

English Explorer and Colonist

Tara Baukus Mello

Arthur M. Schlesinger, jr.
Senior Consulting Editor

Chelsea House Publishers

Philadelphia

Produced by Robert Gerson Publisher's Services, Avondale, PA

CHELSEA HOUSE PUBLISHERS
Editor in Chief Stephen Reginald
Production Manager Pamela Loos
Director of Photography Judy L. Hasday
Art Director Sara Davis
Managing Editor James D. Gallagher

Staff for *JOHN SMITH*
Project Editor Anne Hill
Project Editor/Publishing Coordinator Jim McAvoy
Contributing Editor Amy Handy
Associate Art Director Takeshi Takahashi
Series Design Keith Trego

The Chelsea House World Wide Web address is http://www.chelseahouse.com

3 5 7 9 8 6 4 2

Library of Congress Cataloging-in-Publication Data

Mello, Tara Baukus
John Smith / by Tara Baukus Mello.
   p.   cm. — (Colonial leaders.)
Includes bibliographical references and index.
Summary: A biography of the colonist and explorer who led the struggling
Jamestown colony through its early years and helped found Virginia.
ISBN 0-7910-5345-8 (hc);   ISBN 0-7910-5688-0 (pb)
1. Smith, John, 1580-1631 Juvenile literature.   2. Colonists—Virginia—Jamestown
Biography Juvenile literature.   3. Jamestown (Va.)—History—17th century Juvenile
literature.   4. Jamestown (Va.) Biography Juvenile literature.   5. Virginia—
History—Colonial period, ca. 1600-1775 Juvenile literature.   [1. Smith, John,
1580-1631.   2. Explorers.   3. Jamestown (Va.)—History.   4. Virginia—History—
Colonial period, ca. 1600-1775.]   I. Title.   II. Series.
F229.S7M45   1999
973.2'1'092—dc21
[B]   99-24004
                                                                          CIP

The author wishes to thank Christina Baukus for her invaluable assistance in
researching the life of John Smith and for sharing her knowledge of colonial history.

Publisher's Note: In Colonial and Revolutionary War America, there were no standard rules for spelling, punctuation, capitalization, or grammar. Some of the quotations that appear in the Colonial Leaders and Revolutionary War Leaders series come from original documents and letters written during this time in history. Original quotations reflect writing inconsistencies of the period.

Contents

As an adventurous English boy, John Smith longed to see the world, but he probably never imagined that he'd become famous for helping to settle a new colony. This swashbuckling statue stands in Jamestown, Virginia, where he was an important leader.

Early
Adventures

Almost from the very beginning, John Smith longed for adventure. As a young boy growing up in the town of Willoughby, in Lincolnshire, England, John attended boarding school near his home. There he studied Latin, grammar, composition, and math. His father owned his own farm. When John was born in 1580, it was expected that he would be a farmer like his father, but it was not long before John had his own ideas.

From the earliest days in school, John dreamed of a life at sea. He dreamed of adventure on the great ocean that could be seen from Louth, the town where he attended school. When John was 15, his father allowed him to leave school and become a merchant's **apprentice**. Many boys left school at this age and went to learn different jobs in their apprenticeships.

John moved to King's Lynn, a **seaport** about 50 miles from his home and worked for a **merchant** named Thomas Sendall. His father hoped that John would be happy knowing that he would someday be able to go to sea while working for Mr. Sendall. But young John could hardly wait to see the world and, after his father died in 1596, he quit his apprenticeship.

Although he was just 16 years old, John went off on his first adventure and became a soldier in the Netherlands. He served in the army for three or four years. When he returned to England, he took a job as a servant for Lord Willoughby's sons Peregrine and Robert while they traveled through Europe. Soon the brothers decided they did not need another servant and they gave John enough money to return home to England.

A scene of contemporary Holland shows some
buildings still remaining from the time of John
Smith's travels through the country 400 years ago.

In search of a new adventure, John instead traveled through France, Holland, and Scotland, where he tried to get a position with the court of King James. He was unsuccessful, however, and soon returned to England. Back at home he read books about fighting, studied Italian, and learned horseback riding. Soon John was in search of another adventure and, at age 20, he decided to leave England to see more of the world.

On this trip John decided to join the Austrian army in Hungary to fight the Turks. The trip to Hungary was long and filled with danger. In France he was robbed of all his money and baggage. A **noble** lady helped him and he took a ship from Marseilles, France, to Italy. The ship was caught in a terrible storm. According to John's writings, the other passengers, who were Roman Catholic, did not like him because he was a Protestant and an Englishman. They blamed him for the storm and threw him overboard.

Luckily John did not drown. Instead, he swam to an island and was rescued by another ship the next day. Although a kind Frenchman gave him new clothes and some other belongings, things were not calm for long. While the new ship was sailing across the Mediterranean, they tried to contact another ship from Italy. This ship was not friendly and responded by firing guns at them. The two ships fought until the Italian ship surrendered.

When John arrived in Italy, he spent some time sightseeing. While he was there, he watched Pope Clement VIII say Mass in Rome. Eventually he went to Vienna, Austria, where he enrolled in the army. It had been almost a year since John first left England and decided to join the Austrian army.

It was not long before everyone in the army began to notice John. He taught the senior officers how to use torches to signal other troops. Later he showed General Khissl how to trick the enemy into thinking they had a much larger army. To do this, John lit thousands of matches to imitate lines of soldiers, ready for battle. These techniques helped the Austrians win a battle and John was promoted. His new role was captain and he was in charge of 250 horsemen. From this day in 1601 on, John would forever be known as Captain John Smith.

Many people today think that John Smith was the captain of one of the ships that traveled from England to settle Virginia. John was never a sea captain, but earned his title when he fought in the Austrian army.

John continued to fight in the army, winning more battles and narrowly escaping injury. During one battle his horse was killed underneath him and John had to fight on foot against soldiers on horseback.

One day John became even more famous. It was in a town called Regall, where a commander from the Turkish army, Lord Turbashaw, challenged any captain from the Austrian army to a **joust**. Lord Turbashaw said that the winner of the joust would cut off the loser's head. The officers of the Austrian army **drew lots** to decide who would fight the Turkish lord. John was selected to fight, and he killed Lord Turbashaw only moments after the battle had begun. John cut off the man's head and gave it to his general as a trophy of the fight.

Lord Turbashaw's friend, Grualgo, was upset not only that his friend was dead, but also that an enemy solider had won the joust. Grualgo challenged John to another fight the next day. John won this battle, killing Grualgo with a shot from his pistol. He cut off Grualgo's head and gave that to his general as well. By this time John was feeling very important and he challenged anyone in the Turkish army to battle. A man named Bonny Mulgro accepted, and John killed and beheaded him also.

After this battle, John was seen as a hero among the people in his army. He received a promotion, a new horse, a sword, and a very expensive belt. His boss, the general, even hugged him. Soon afterward, Prince Zsigmond of Transylvania awarded John an **insignia** of the three Turk's heads, a picture of the prince in a gold frame, and a pay raise for his great victory.

The battle with the Turks was not over, and soon the Turks began winning. Nearly 30,000 soldiers in the Austrian army died. John was severely hurt and was left by the Turks to die. He was captured and sold as a slave. John and the other slaves were forced to march 500 miles to Constantinople (which is known today as Istanbul) and his owner made him a slave to a lady John named Charatza Tragabigzanda. The lady liked John and learned about his adventures, since they both spoke Italian. Trying to be kind, the lady sent him to her brother in Tartary and asked that he be treated well.

But the man treated John poorly. In fact, as soon as he arrived in Tartary, his head and beard were shaved, his clothes were taken, and an iron ring was fastened around his neck. Because John was the last of the slaves to arrive, he was "slave of slaves to them all," as he wrote. He was forced to work many hours and was not given much

The immense mosque of Hagia Sophia towers
over Istanbul. The city was called Constantinople
when John Smith was brought there as a slave.

food. One day John was working on one of the most distant fields with his master. The man began to beat him for no reason and John struck back using his **thresher** as a club. John killed the man instantly.

When he realized that he could now be free, he dressed in his master's clothes and rode off on his horse. After a few weeks of wandering the countryside, a governor from Muscovy removed the iron ring from around his neck and John then began searching for the commanders of his army. When he found them, Prince Zsigmond felt bad for everything John had been through. He gave John a lot of money and allowed him to leave the army.

It was time to head back to England but, as he always seemed to do, first John decided to do some sightseeing. He traveled again through Germany, France, Spain, and North Africa. He became a passenger on a French ship that ended up in battle with two Spanish ships. For two days the three ships battled, until finally

the French ship was able to get safely to port.
From there John went home to England, where
he discovered that England had changed a lot
in the previous four years.

In the last decade of his life, John Smith published one of the very first manuals for sailors. Here, as part of a floating exhibit in modern-day Jamestown, a performer demonstrates life aboard a colonial vessel.

Journey to Jamestown

While John was away on his latest adventure, Queen Elizabeth I had died and King James Stuart had inherited the throne. More important, the English had become interested in traveling to America again. It had been about 15 years since the last group had tried unsuccessfully to settle in America at Roanoke, Virginia, and the English were ready to try again.

The English wanted to settle a new colony in America for many reasons. The colonies, the English thought, would bring them many riches from the unusual fruits, herbs, and other raw materials (like gold) that were there. They also thought they would find a river that led to the Pacific Ocean in order to make a quicker route to Asia and India, where they could buy spices and silks. They called this route the Northwest Passage.

The English were not the only people who wanted to build colonies in America. The Spanish had already settled where Florida and Georgia are today and had been very successful. The English were afraid that the Spanish would continue to take over America, so they were anxious to get there to build a new colony. In 1605 the Virginia Company was formed by a group of knights and merchants to arrange a trip to America to start a new colony.

The Virginia Company was a business called a joint stock company. This meant that people invested money in the business. In return they received a portion of the profits and the right to make decisions about the business. The English government, who granted the charter to the company, also received some of the profits from the business.

The 1606 seal of the King's Council for the Colony of Virginia shows a portrait of King James I.

Joint stock companies were very popular in England by this time, but no one had ever formed one for a new colony. In 1605 the Virginia Company, also known as the London Company, and one other business, called the Plymouth Company, were started for this reason. Because the government and the stockholders did not have to invest a lot of money, this was a way for the colonies to be built without any one person having to take a big risk.

In the hopes of making money in America,

144 men agreed to sail to Virginia. These men were employees of the Virginia Company. They had to work for seven years in the new colony and at the end, they would receive land in the colony as their payment. In return for their seven years of employment, the men received their passage on the ship, as well as food and supplies to build their own shelter and to protect themselves. Many of the men on the first Virginia Company voyage left families at home in England.

John, who was ready to begin another adventure, joined the Virginia Company. He spent about a year working with the men who would lead the voyage to America. In December 1606 three ships—the *Susan Constant,* the *Godspeed,* and the *Discovery*—left England. It had taken three weeks for the group to sail out of the harbor because the wind was blowing in the wrong direction.

When they left, the Virginia Company gave them a set of instructions to be opened in Virginia, which named the men who would be in

The wooden sailing ships of the 17th century
were much more elaborately decorated than the
streamlined steel vessels of today.

charge of the colony when they arrived. During the trip the captain of each ship was in charge. Captain Christopher Newport sailed the *Susan Constant.* Although he had only one arm, he was an experienced sailor who had fought in many sea raids with the Spanish. Captain Bartholomew Gosnold, who sailed the *Godspeed,* had a lot of experience sailing to America. No one knows very much about Captain John Ratcliffe, who sailed the *Discovery,* except that he was known for getting himself into trouble.

There is no complete list of the passengers on the three ships, but from John's books we know some of the occupations of the men. They included a reverend, four carpenters, 12 laborers, two bricklayers, a blacksmith, a mason, a tailor, a surgeon, a sail maker, and a drummer.

The journey to Virginia was long and uncomfortable. The passengers were crammed together in the 'tween deck. The air smelled bad and there was no privacy. The food did

This jolly performer reenacting life on a 17th-century ship is probably a lot more cheerful than the original passengers, who had to travel under very difficult conditions, with poor food and cramped quarters.

not last for long and there was not much of it to go around. Passengers, including John, ate salted meat and fish, stale biscuits, spoiled cheese and butter, and drank beer. There was not enough fresh water to drink or cook with. Since the food was so poor, many passengers did not get the proper vitamins they needed and so they had very little energy. Some passengers got very sick, but just one passenger died.

Although most voyages to America took less than two months, the Virginia expedition lasted more than four months. The three ships stopped seven times to get fresh food and supplies and to explore. The men enjoyed these stops, for it was the only time they were able to escape the dullness of traveling by ship.

> The 'tween deck, where the passengers on the voyage to Virginia stayed, was the deck between the main deck where the sailors worked and the cargo hold. It was not very comfortable—there were no rooms and it had very low ceilings. On two of the three ships that sailed on this journey, the ceiling on this deck was less than three feet high.

Things, however, were not dull for John Smith. The first stop they made was in the Canary Islands, and by then John was under arrest. No one knows why John was in trouble, but by the time they stopped at Nevis, an island in the West Indies, John's enemies wanted to hang him from a handmade **gallows**. It was Captain Newport who saved John. He refused to hang him without more evidence. Captain Newport kept John under arrest for the rest of the trip and said that they would look at the evidence when they arrived in Virginia.

On April 26, 1607, the three ships arrived in Chesapeake Bay, on the Virginia coast. Opening the box with the sealed instructions, the men learned that they were supposed to choose the river that seemed to run farthest into the land and find a spot to build the settlement. The instructions also told the men to try to choose a river that originated in a lake and traveled northwest, for the English thought that this would lead to the Pacific Ocean.

When the three ships landed at Jamestown they had no idea what to expect in the new land, so they organized a search party to begin exploring.

The instructions said that seven men would run Jamestown. The captains of the three ships were among this group. The other men were

Edward Maria Wingfield, Captain John Martin, Captain George Kendall, and John Smith. The instructions told the men to choose a president to lead the group. Edward Wingfield was chosen and his first official act was to exclude John from the council, since John was still in trouble.

For the most part the new colonists were happy with the area that would be their new home. The weather was similar to the climate in Spain, with mild temperatures and warm winds. The river was wide and long and could be navigated easily. There was lots of seafood for the men to eat. There were giant crabs, oysters, and mussels and many salt water fish. There were lots of animals on the land too, including some the men had never seen before, such as raccoons and opossums.

For the next several weeks the group explored the area, searching for a good place to build their settlement. Since no Europeans had explored the area, the colonists did not know what they would find. Captain Newport organized a small group to

The Native Americans had customs that seemed
very strange to the colonists, just as their tradi-
tions must have appeared very unusual to the
Indians. John Smith was one of the first to
establish an understanding with them. He is
seen here next to the fire observing a Native
American ritual.

travel up the river to search for minerals and the East Indian Sea. Although he was still in trouble, John was allowed to go on the expedition.

Within four days the group had traveled up the river and into the territory of the Powhatan Indian tribe. These first meetings with the Native Americans were friendly and the men were allowed to visit their villages. After one week of traveling Captain Newport and his men had gone as far as they could go in their ship, so they returned to Jamestown.

When the group arrived, they learned that Jamestown had been attacked by a group of about 200 Indians and two of the colonists were injured. The Indians were scared off when someone fired a small cannon from the *Godspeed,* which was anchored just off the shore. This would be just one of many encounters the new colonists would have with the Native Americans.

Engraved by J.C. Buttre New York.

POCAHONTAS.

Stories about Pocahontas, the daughter of the Powhatan chief, generally imply she was at least a teenager when she met John Smith, but she was actually about 12 years old.

The Powhatan Tribe

When the colonists began to settle Jamestown, Indians had already been living in the area for thousands of years. To the English, the Native Americans seemed like savages who wore odd clothes, if any at all, and who looked very different than they did. The Indians saw the English in much the same way. Because the groups spoke different languages, communication was difficult and many times there were misunderstandings.

The Indians who lived closest to the Jamestown settlement were a tribe called the Powhatans. John Smith was one of the first Englishmen to build a relationship with the Powhatans, including their leader,

Powhatan, and one of his daughters, Pocahontas. One of the main reasons that the English began to establish a relationship with them was for food. The English did not have a good food supply and needed food to feed the new colonists. By this time John had been appointed the supply officer, which meant that it was his responsibility to get the food and other supplies the colonists needed to survive. John began trading with the tribe to get food, although sometimes this was not entirely friendly.

The first major encounter John had with the Powhatans was in the winter of the colonists' first year at Jamestown. John had led several expeditions to explore the area around the settlement and, in December, the council decided that John should take a trip up the Chickahominy River in the hope that it would lead to the mysterious Northwest Passage their superiors wanted them to find. John left with nine men on a **barge** and traveled 27 miles up the river, until there were too many fallen trees for their big boat to continue.

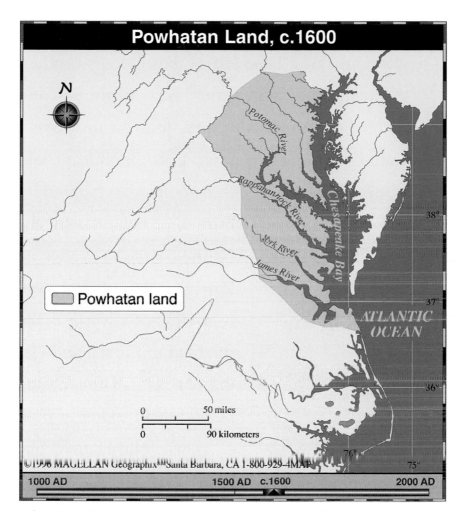

Powhatan Land, c.1600

N

Potomac River

Rappahannock River

York River

James River

Chesapeake Bay

38°

Powhatan land

37°

ATLANTIC
OCEAN

36°

| 0 | | 50 miles |
| 0 | | 90 kilometers |

©1996 MAGELLAN Geographix℠ Santa Barbara, CA 1-800-929-4MAP

76°

75°

1000 AD   1500 AD   c.1600   2000 AD

The Powhatan Confederacy, led by the Algonquin chief Powhatan, covered an area of land along the East Coast, from what is now Maryland to Virginia.

John, two of his men, and two Native American guides continued in a canoe about 20 miles farther up the river. While out exploring the area, John and a guide were attacked by the Pamunkeys, a tribe led by Powhatan's brother, Opechancanough. John was captured and brought to meet with him. John, who spoke a bit of their language, tried to communicate with Opechancanough. Opechancanough tried to learn more about why the "white men" were in Powhatan's country and John tried to learn if the river led to the sea and was the shortcut to the Orient he had been trying to find.

Unlike the English and other Europeans, the Powhatan tribe did not write anything down. The only way that they communicated was through speaking and gestures. In the 1600s, all the stories about the Powhatans were written by the English, who did not always understand the tribe's customs or language.

When John learned that there was a body of salt water about five days' walk away and that the Indians were planning to attack Jamestown again, he asked Opechancanough to let him send a message back to the Jamestown people. Opechancanough, who did not understand how a piece of paper could hold such a detailed message, agreed. When the Native

Americans who delivered the message returned, Opechancanough was convinced that John was a magician and a **werowance**. As a result, Opechancanough decided to bring John to the great leader, Powhatan.

When John was brought to Powhatan's hut, he was allowed to wash and then many different food dishes were laid out in front of him. While he ate, there was a long conversation between Powhatan and the elder tribesmen. Then two big stones were carried in and John was forced to lie on them. According to John's writings later, several Powhatans stood over him with clubs, as if they were going to kill him. Suddenly, a little girl ran from the Great Powhatan's side to John and placed her head over his, as if to protect him from the blows. The Native Americans put down their clubs and the little girl helped John up. Pocahontas, one of Powhatan's daughters, had saved him.

Although we will never really know for sure what happened, history experts think that

Pocahontas Saving the Life of John Smith.

Pocahontas is said to have saved the life of Captain John Smith more than once, most famously when some elder tribesman seemed about to kill him. However, some say that may have been part of a special ceremony to make him part of the tribe.

Powhatan never meant to kill John. They believe that this was just a ceremony to induct John into the tribe. Just the same, John did not know this and for the rest of his life, he thought of the young girl named Pocahontas as the person who saved him from death.

At the end of the ceremony, Powhatan made John the werowance of the village of Capahowasic. He said that they would now be friends and that John could stay at the village whenever he wanted.

A few days after John was allowed to return to Jamestown, a large fire almost destroyed it. It was January and, in the cold, it was hard for the colonists to rebuild the settlement. Soon Powhatan sent deer, bread, and raccoon skins to the colonists. A few days later he sent more gifts, and this time Pocahontas delivered them.

As time passed, more colonists began to arrive and everyone was allowed to trade with the Powhatan tribe. Captain Newport sent gifts to Powhatan, and one day Powhatan sent word that he wanted John to bring Captain Newport to meet him. In February John and Captain Newport embarked on their journey to see

Powhatan with about 30 men and two of Powhatan's guides. When they arrived, Powhatan and his men were nice to their guests. Captain Newport presented Powhatan with a young man named Thomas Savage, who was to stay with him as a sign of the colonists' friendship. Powhatan gave his servant Namontack to Captain Newport as a sign of his friendship. Each man would learn the other group's language and that would help them communicate.

History experts think that Powhatan was so nice to John and Captain Newport because he was trying to learn why the English had come to Virginia and when they were going to leave. The colonists were nice to the Powhatans because they thought that the tribe could lead them to the Northwest Passage, share with them other secrets of the land, and give them food.

For the next several months the colonists and the Powhatans were friendly. They traded supplies and food and Pocahontas often made visits to Jamestown during the trading. John became friends with Pocahontas, who was about 12 years old. He liked her because she was happy and not always complaining like many of the colonists. Pocahontas liked John because he was cheerful and always treated her and her people well, unless someone was trying to cheat him.

The colonists and the Powhatans got along well when each group did what the other group wanted. This meant that when the colonists asked for something that the tribe did not want to give or vice versa, there was trouble. Once, when John refused to give the Native Americans the swords they had requested, they tried to steal them. John captured seven Powhatans and was ready to do battle with the rest of the tribe until Powhatan apologized.

About six months later, John tried to force the Powhatans to give the colonists corn and when he went to Powhatan's country to retrieve it, John and his men were not welcomed. Powhatan felt threatened by the white men and ordered his people to attack. Pocahontas saved

John Smith is seen here giving a carved wooden doll
to a Native American woman, probably Pocahontas.
After a while relations between the colonists and the
Powhatans fell apart.

John and his men by warning them of the attack. It was the last time that Pocahontas saw John in America.

By 1609 the relationship with the Powhatans was so poor that John, now president of the council, could trade with the Indians only by force. Because of this, the colonists did not starve over the winter, but it also meant the relationship with the Indians was damaged forever. It was not long before the Native Americans' anger toward the colonists turned into hatred.

Pocahontas, then about 13 years old, was no longer allowed to visit Jamestown. The Powhatans saw the colonists as people who were only out for their own good and who did not really care about the tribe at all. As far as the Powhatans were concerned, the colonists were not friends but people to be avoided.

The original settlement at Jamestown has been re-created in the 20th century, complete with actors dressed as settlers. Modern-day visitors can experience life as it was in the colonies.

A Leader at Jamestown

From his earliest days of traveling in Europe, John was used to being a leader, not a follower. When he joined the Virginia Company, it seemed that he hoped to be named as one of the members of the council who would lead the Jamestown colonists. Although we know from the charter that John was named to the council, he was not allowed to take his position when the ships arrived. But in June John was allowed to join the council, and in August supply officer Thomas Stoodie died, and John took over his duties.

As the supply officer, John had the job of gathering all the supplies and distributing them to the colonists as they were needed. John had created the program to trade with the Native Americans for food. Because of his policy, the colonists were able to get enough food to survive. He also organized the colonists in the daily duties of the settlement, including planting crops and preparing lumber to ship to England. These things were not really part of his job as a supply officer—he just did them because they needed to get done.

But John was an adventurer and he often led expeditions to the areas surrounding Jamestown. On one expedition, John led his men up the shore and into the Potomac River, where they tried to catch fish for food and to trade. The large numbers of fish in the waters surprised the group, who used some odd fishing techniques, since they did not have any nets. John wrote, "in divers places that aboundance of fish lying with their heads above the water, as for the want of nets (our barge driving amongst them) we attempted to catch them with a frying pan." Although frying pans had much longer handles than they do today, it was still a very odd thing to use to catch fish. And it did not work very well. When the boat moved to shallow waters later, they used their swords to spear the fish. The men discovered that this was a better way to catch fish and they speared more fish in an hour than they could eat. It was during this trip that John learned that some fish were not as nice as others. He caught a stingray, which drove its long tail into his arm. It hurt so much that John thought he was going to die and told his men to dig him a grave.

When John returned from this trip, many of the colonists were sick. The settlement was a disaster and Captain Ratcliffe, the president of the council, was not doing a good job of keeping things together. John made him step down and appointed himself president, and the other council members agreed to the change. They did not like John's harsh style of leadership, but they knew that he would do a good job and help solve their problems.

Since John and his men had no nets, they tried inventive ways to catch fish. On one trip John made the mistake of catching a stingray, which stung him badly.

The Powhatans continued to trade with John out of fear of what he would do if they did not. Although John did not treat the Native Americans very well, he was the only one who always got the food the colonists needed. Many times John paid for the food he took.

By the spring of 1609 the colony was running more smoothly. The rebuilding of the village after the fire was progressing. The men had constructed houses and put new roofs on the church and the storehouse. They were beginning to grow some of their own food, including corn. The colonists made their own tar, soap, and glass and learned how to weave their own fishing nets.

Things were very good in Jamestown until John discovered that rats had spoiled their entire storage of corn. The colonists would not have enough food to last until the next crop was ready to be picked. John decided to split up the colonists, which was the only way he thought they could survive. A small group went to Point Comfort, where there were fish to eat, while another group went to the waterfalls on the James River. A third group went downriver, where they could gather oysters.

Being president of the council was not an easy job. Many of the colonists did not realize how hard it would be to settle a new colony, so when they arrived, they did not want to work. They believed that they should only do the types of jobs they were used to doing at home. For example, soldiers did not want to do the jobs of civilians and skilled gentlemen did not want to do manual labor. Also, most of the colonists did not want to hunt and fish for their own food. They were lazy and preferred to trade their belongings with the Powhatans for food. John would not let them do this and he forced the men to gather their own food.

John convinced the men to work partly by threatening them and partly by working hard himself. He thought that if others saw him building houses and planting they would help too. Using his military experience, John divided the men into small groups and rotated their jobs regularly, so no one had to do one job for very long. Every Saturday John gathered some of the most fit men and brought them to Smithfield, a large field near Jamestown. He taught them how to

Not all the settlers at Jamestown were willing to work hard to make the colony a success. Captain John Smith had to convince them all to pitch in.

march, how to perform military maneuvers, and how to use a **musket**. Sometimes the Native Americans watched while the men would practice by shooting at trees.

The colonists were not very happy about the way John led Jamestown, but they could not vote him out of office because the other council members had died. Everyone knew that there were new instructions coming from the Virginia Company in London and that it would probably change John's role as president. But the ship had not arrived, and no one knew what the instructions were. John had many enemies, including Captain Ratcliffe, whom he had forced out of office the year before. His enemies decided that they had enough power to force him to step down as president.

According to John's writings, he waited until his year as president was over and then appointed Captain John Martin. John said that the man resigned within just a few hours of being appointed and he was forced to hold office for several more weeks.

John continued with his duties and one day, when he was sailing back from the settlement

Back in England, the Virginia Company used posters like this one to advertise trips to its colony in the New World.

at the falls of the James River, the bag of gun powder that he had been carrying exploded and wounded his leg badly. Reports are not clear if this was an accident or if one of John's men was trying to hurt him. Although John was injured severely, he was able to throw himself overboard to put out his burning clothes. The crew helped him back into the boat and they returned to Jamestown.

During John's time, there were no rules for spelling, punctuation, capitalization, or grammar. People just spelled the words out the way they thought they sounded. Sometimes the same person spelled a word several different ways in the same document.

As John laid in bed trying to recover from his leg injury, he was worn out. The colonists were no longer listening to him and he knew that his term as president was about to end. Then he heard that Captain Ratcliffe and some of John's enemies were planning to murder him. John wrote about himself, ". . . seeing the President, unable to stand, and neere bereft of his senses by reason of his torment, they had plotted to have murdered him in his bed. But his heart did faile him that should have given fire to that mercilesse Pistoll."

It seems from John's writings that a man had come to his room to kill him, but then either he changed his mind or his pistol did not work properly. Just the same, John got the message that he was not wanted in Jamestown anymore and he made arrangements to leave on the next ship. John left Virginia in September 1609 to return to his home in England.

The 17th century is sometimes called the Age of Exploration, since many ships from a number of different countries set out to discover more about the world and to establish new settlements.

Later Travels

F or the first few years John was home in
England, not much is known about what he
did, except that he was one of the people who
helped write a book called *A Map of Virginia*. The
book, which was published in 1612, included John's
description of the events that happened in Virginia
in the last few years before he left. John's map of
Virginia was also included and it was used for
many years. As time passed, he thought less about
Virginia and began to wonder about the area north
of there.

In 1614 John was given two ships and he sailed to
Maine. During this trip John realized that there were

many codfish in the waters and much **sassafras** on the land. The area had many excellent ports and John thought that these qualities made the area a good place to start a new colony that could be very profitable for the English. John gave names to many of the areas he encountered and some of them remain today. It is because of John Smith that the northeastern states are known as New England. Although John did not invent the word *Massachusetts* (it was the name of a Native American tribe), John began calling that area Massachusetts and the name stuck.

After John landed in Maine, he traveled south to explore. Since he thought the area would make a good colony, he made careful maps and sketches. He traded goods for furs to bring back to England, but his main interest was in studying the area so he could make a good map when he returned home. Because of John's explorations of this area, the Plymouth Company named John the "Admiral of New

England," a title that made him very proud.

When John returned to England he met Sir Ferdinando Gorges, a member of the Plymouth Company, and they decided to build a colony in New England. It was hard for them to raise the money they needed to travel. Investors were willing to give money for expeditions that were going to fish, to look for gold, or to trade, but they were not willing to give money to help a colony get started. Finally they got the money they needed and in the spring of 1615, John was ready to set sail.

Unfortunately, John's ship was not built very well and he had to turn around before he had gotten very far. He got another ship as quickly as he could and set out again on June 24, 1615. But John and his men had not been traveling long before they encountered a pirate ship. Although it seems the pirates left them alone, the ship only sailed a short distance before two more pirate ships caught up with the ship and told John to surrender. John was able to sail away unharmed.

One day later, John and his men encountered four French **man-of-war** ships, whose sailors captured John's men and stole many of their supplies. After about a week the men were released and all their belongings were returned, except for their weapons. John was determined to continue on the journey, but his men did not agree and left John on one of the French pirate ships. He was a prisoner on the ship for several months and used the time to begin writing another book. This book was about his trip to New England the year before.

One stormy night John climbed into the ship's rowboat with his book and escaped. The wind and the rain made the sea fierce. John rowed the boat and then bailed the water out of it all night. Finally he landed on the shore in France very tired, but free from his captors. By December he had returned to England, where he began looking for someone to publish his new book, *A Description of New England.*

In addition to the descriptions of New England in this book, John also included a map of

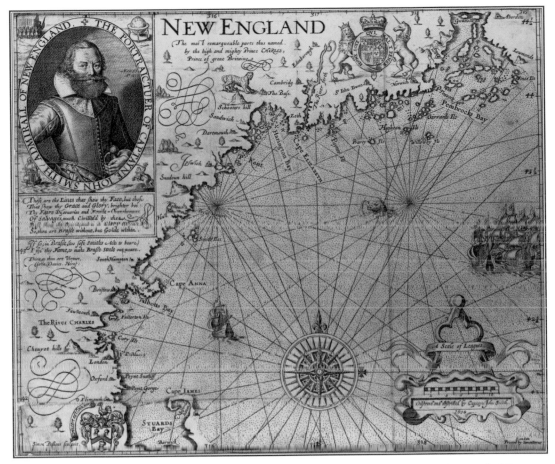

After his adventures in Virginia, John Smith explored New England. He later wrote of those travels and published this map, which includes his portrait.

the area. The map is very accurate and looks much like New England today. Also included in the book is a portrait of John, which is the only known picture of him.

While John was working on publishing his latest book, he was also searching for someone to invest in his idea of a colony in New England. He needed to find someone who could give him enough money so he could set sail again. Just as John's book was being printed, he learned that Pocahontas was in London. She had married an Englishman named John Rolfe and they had a baby son named Thomas.

When John heard of Pocahontas's arrival in England, he went to visit her. Pocahontas was so surprised to see John that she did not speak. Everyone left her alone for a while and later, John returned by himself. Pocahontas and he were not very comfortable and they talked for only a short time. This was the last time that they saw each other, for Pocahontas died less than a year later.

After his visit with Pocahontas, John continued to search for someone to invest in the colony that he wanted to build in New England. John was finally able to get three ships ready to

Back in England, John learned that Pocahontas had come to London as the wife of an English colonist named John Rolfe. Smith and Pocahontas met briefly in London, for the last time.

sail on another voyage to America. Just as the ships were about to leave, strong winds started blowing and no ships could sail out of the harbor. The winds blew for three months and eventually the expedition was canceled. John kept trying to find a way to get to America to start his colony. While he searched for an investor, he wrote more books about his adventures in America.

John was interested in starting colonies in America not only because he thought it would be good for England, but also because he needed a job. In 1620 John learned about the group who called themselves Pilgrims and how they planned to start a colony in New England. John tried to get them to hire him, but they hired a young captain named Miles Standish and they bought John's books and maps instead.

In April 1621 another man named John Smyth, which was pronounced Smith, suggested to the stockholders of the London Company that someone should write the history of America. John Smith decided he should be the author.

John tried to find work helping the Pilgrims set up their colony in New England, but they used his writings instead of him. Here they hold their first sermon after landing at Plymouth.

While John was gathering information for his book, some very important news arrived. The ship *Seaflower* had just reached England with the news that the Native Americans in Virginia had killed 347 colonists. The London Company sent supplies and weapons as soon as they learned of the attack. John asked the London Company to allow him to sail back to Virginia with soldiers to fight the Native Americans, but he was ignored.

John continued to write his book on the history of America and finished it in 1624. *The Generall Historie of Virginia, New-England, and the Summer Isles* was the most important book that he wrote. For the first time, people began to pay more attention to John and his ideas.

For the next few years John published several books, including a manual for sailors, which was the only book of its type for many years. Then he spent a couple of years writing a book about all of his adventures, including the very earliest ones as a soldier in the army. This book is often called *True Travels*, a shortened name for the original title, which had 22 words. John had just become ill when his last book, which was about how to farm in America, was published.

Barely able to sign his name on his will, John Smith died in London on June 21, 1631. Although he spent more time in England and Europe than he did in America, it was the American colonies that he loved. He wrote that "they have been my wife, my hawks, my hounds, my cards, my dice, and in total my best content."

GLOSSARY

apprentice an inexperienced person who learns a skill or trade from an expert

barge a large flat-bottomed boat

colony a group of people living in a new territory that is governed by their parent country

drawing lots a process to choose a person or thing in a fair manner

gallows a frame of two posts and a crossbeam that is used to hang criminals

insignia a badge or emblem of honor

joust to fight on horseback with a lance as a weapon

man-of-war a type of ship used for combat

merchant a storekeeper

musket a large, heavy gun usually carried on a soldier's shoulder

noble a person of higher class; an aristocrat

sassafras a type of tree whose root bark was used as a flavoring and was once thought to have medicinal properties

seaport a harbor or coastal town where ships can dock

thresher a tool used to separate the seeds from a plant

werowance a male chief of a tribe

CHRONOLOGY

1580 John Smith is born in the town of Willoughby in Lincolnshire, England.

1595 John becomes an apprentice for merchant Thomas Sendall in King's Lynn, Norfolk, England.

1596 John's father, George, dies and John leaves his apprenticeship in search of adventure.

1597–99 John becomes an English soldier and fights in the Netherlands.

1601 John joins the Austrian army, helps win several battles, and is promoted to captain.

1602 He beheads three Turks and is named a hero. Later he is captured and sold as a slave.

1606 John embarks on the first expedition of the Virginia Company in December.

1607 John and the rest of the passengers on the three ships arrive in Virginia in April; he is captured by the Powhatans in December and is saved from death by Pocahontas.

1608 John brings Captain Newport to meet Powhatan; John is sworn in as president of the council in September.

CHRONOLOGY

1609 John continues his expeditions and the running of Jamestown until he is wounded in a gunpowder explosion. He leaves for England in September.

1610–12 John Smith writes and publishes *A Map of Virginia*.

1614 John sails to America and explores Maine and Massachusetts. He returns to England and is named the "Admiral of New England," for his explorations of the area.

1615 John sets out to start a colony in New England but his ship is unfit for the trip. On his second try, his ship is captured by pirates. After escaping he returns to England to write *A Description of New England*.

1616 John sees Pocahontas while she is visiting England.

1620–31 John publishes six books, mostly about his experiences in America.

1631 John dies on June 21 in London.

COLONIAL TIME LINE

1607 Jamestown, Virginia, is settled by the English.

1620 Pilgrims on the *Mayflower* land at Plymouth, Massachusetts.

1623 The Dutch settle New Netherland, the colony that later becomes New York.

1630 Massachusetts Bay Colony is started.

1634 Maryland is settled as a Roman Catholic colony. Later Maryland becomes a safe place for people with different religious beliefs.

1636 Roger Williams is thrown out of the Massachusetts Bay Colony. He settles Rhode Island, the first colony to give people freedom of religion.

1682 William Penn forms the colony of Pennsylvania.

1688 Pennsylvania Quakers make the first formal protest against slavery.

1692 Trials for witchcraft are held in Salem, Massachusetts.

COLONIAL TIME LINE

1712   Slaves revolt in New York. Twenty-one blacks are killed as punishment.

1720   Major smallpox outbreak occurs in Boston. Cotton Mather and some doctors try a new treatment. Many people think the new treatment shouldn't be used.

1754   French and Indian War begins. It ends nine years later.

1761   Benjamin Banneker builds a wooden clock that keeps precise time.

1765   Britain passes the Stamp Act. Violent protests break out in the colonies. The Stamp Act is ended the next year.

1775   The battles of Lexington and Concord begin the American Revolution.

1776   Declaration of Independence is signed.

FURTHER READING

Brown, Gene. *Discovery and Settlement: Europe Meets The New World* (1490–1700). New York: Twenty First Century Books, 1995.

Hume, Ivor Noel. *The Virginia Adventure.* New York: Alfred A. Knopf, 1994.

Knight, James E. Jamestown: *A New World Adventure.* Mahwah, N.J.: Troll Press, 1998.

Moscinski, Sharon. *Tracing Our English Roots.* Santa Fe: John Muir Publications, 1995.

Nee, Kay Bonner. *Powhatan: The Story of an American Indian.* Minneapolis: Dillon Press, 1971.

Sakurai, Gail. *The Jamestown Colony.* New York: Children's Press, 1997.

Tunis, Edwin. *Colonial Living.* Baltimore: Johns Hopkins University Press, 1999.

INDEX

INDEX

PICTURE CREDITS

ABOUT THE AUTHOR

TARA BAUKUS MELLO has published more than 1000 articles in newspapers and magazines and has written six books for children. She is also the author of *George Washington,* part of the Revolutionary Leaders series. A graduate of Harvard University, Tara grew up on Cape Cod, Massachusetts. She now lives in southern California with her husband, Jeff, and their dog, Tyler.

Senior Consulting Editor **ARTHUR M. SCHLESINGER, JR.** is the leading American historian of our time. He won the Pulitzer Prize for his book *The Age of Jackson* (1945) and again for *A Thousand Days* (1965). This chronicle of the Kennedy Administration also won a National Book Award. He has written many other books including a multi-volume series, *The Age of Roosevelt*. Professor Schlesinger is the Albert Schweitzer Professor of the Humanities at the City University of New York, and has been involved in several other Chelsea House projects, including the REVOLUTIONARY WAR LEADERS biographies on the most prominent figures of early American history.